AF446594

.

"Out of all the weapons in the world, I chose poetry"

A little bit about me before you start this fantasy parade.

Storytelling has been a big part of my life. These poems are no less than a story in itself. Are they fictionlised? Absolutely but they do tell a story on how it should've been for me and how it can be still! Poetry, I never realised it'll play a big part in my life that I've a book of my own. If it wasn't for her - I believe - this book wouldn't have existed. So if you're a poet in love - let the one know before poems is all you have on your side. I mean, that's not a bad thing too, I guess! Poetry gives you the freedom to immortalised your love, a freedom that nobody can take it away. The only homeland that will remains yours until the very end!

Wait, I thought I was going to tell you guys about myself? Okaaaaay! That didn't go as planned - well what does anyway?

Hope you all enjoy these poems!

Love, P!

Dedicated to the ones who have all this love
but have no idea where to put it

poetry, fiction and me // 1

started writing at 2.19 am

while fourth of july

playing in the background

"We're all gonna die"

And yet this line gives me hope

a hope in what? I am yet to understand

followed by sprite by coin

"I don't know where to go

so I'm coming home"

a place that doesn't exist for me

but what about new york?

that still yet to be my reality

now sprite by coin is on the loop

been months since I heard it

heart needed to hear it

but mind always reminded me of it

a song that feels like home

that reminds me of myself where

poetry, fiction and me

made a world together

so maybe I'm a fantasy parade

and I am yet to wake up from

reality that I'm awake in

where it's 2.38 am now and I played

time is dancing by ben howard

a song that saved me

that keeps me alive when

I have no reason to

"lost in insignificane of mine

I had no words to say"

and here I am,

eager to say more

eager to write more

"Hold it in here,

let's go dancing

I do believe we're only

passing through"

it's turning out more of

lyrics of different songs

than a poem but I guess

this is my heart needed

after a long time

it's 2.44 am now and

I have to wake up early

but my eyes insist to stay open

the heart denies to slow it's heartbeat

maybe because I'm writing a poem for me

poetry, fiction and me

maybe it's not a bad idea afterall

poetry where my fictional world exists

and me, the one who seeks love

as the reality disfigured me for it

I doubt if anyone reads up to this point

but the poem belongs to me

so even if anyone didn't

it kept my heart kind

which was the whole point

is this a another sleepless night?

I haven't had that in a while

often turning into rare

I guess for my heart it's fair

but is the mind restful?

got any vacancy to think?

I'll say it's upside down

but to be honest I haven't gotten

any time for my mind to think

so I'll let it rest now

keep my phone aside now

It's 2.54 am now

while time is dancing on the loop

poetry, fiction and me

that's the world I live in

and I guess I'm stuck in that loop

so I'll rest now, for the hours I got

and the poem won't be long

it'll wrap up in few mintues

thats what I thought

3.00 am

Sweet Nothing

Heart felt peace after a long time

maybe because we didn't meet for a long time

I always thought peace had only one definition

Meeting you changed it in a different motion

and I realised I crave for this peace even more

Hopefully it will last more

and as we shared stories

we laughed in between

cherry on a margherita pizza?

that was my favorite part

and I realised you don't like them on pizza

as you put them apart

and as we walked out of the cafe

should I hold her hand? I hoped

but couldn't dare to

as I need more reasons to see you

holding your hand will be one of them

and to walk pass the flower shop

a sunflower to give, was meant to be

heart felt peace as it saw you smile

and we went our own ways

where you told me

I missed my chocolates from you

another reason to see you

the list gets bigger

which puts smile on my face

and as i got into the bus

I figured what would be the best way to end this evening

sweet nothing from taylor swift

"on the way home

I wrote a poem

you said, what a mind

this happens all the time"

only in this part, I wrote a poem

as I layed down on the bed

hoping this is where I end the poem

well, atleast that's what I said

as I know it'll continue even more

to write about how the sky was pink on my way home

where my heart felt peace

and I walked till home

hoping for more.

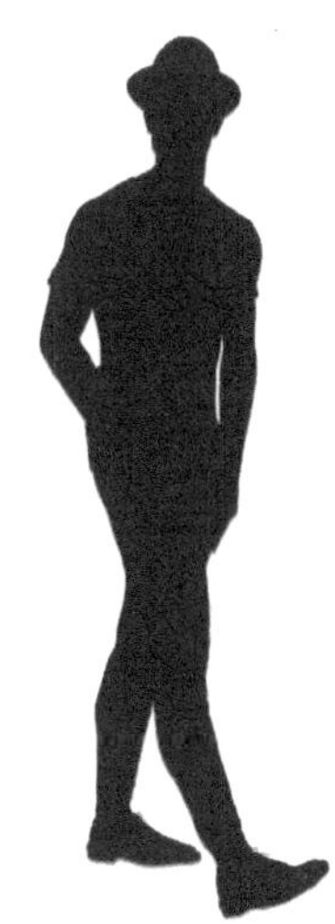

You Won

heart eyes, they won me over a long time ago

but heartbreak followed me back

It still haunts me even if it was long time ago

years passed by and I stood to the other side of the door

waiting for you to open it

only to realise it was never meant for me

to be opened

you won, at making me move away

from the other side of the door

I walked away with ease and confused

as how it became so easy to walk away

from a place where I stood for years of time

and I realised all I needed is time

yes, you won, I no longer feel

the love I used to

how do I know?

your name does not appear first anymore now

when all i did is wrote it wherever I go

would I fall back again?

I don't know now

I am outside the void of love

I am in light but the irony is, it still feels empty

before all I did is mention you in my dreams

and now all they have is a fading sound

which I cannot hear anymore

so yeah, you won,

I am falling out of it

but here I am writing another poem on your name

because when i painted my whole world by you

I never thought of erasing it

but I'm learning it

knowing my ways to erase it

knowing that one day

my heart won't have the place on your name,

that once I felt peace for having

but my heart made me realise,

erasing you will have a price to pay

It won't let anyone else have a home in it

that's all I can say

Does It Mention You?

a poem that I've been trying to write

it mentions you in every possible way

like a sunny summer with a glass of lemonade

rather than netflix, old rom coms on a vhs player

but I realised the poem haven't mentioned you yet

well, it did, actually.

as it won't feel the same if it wasn't for you being beside me

songs on loop as we dance away our problems for a time

while we dance, I stop for a few seconds of time

to believe in the moment,

that I see you infront me

that in this world, you belong to me

your hugs, headbumps, and kisses

exists for my heart so it can stay kind

so tell me, the poem that I've been trying to write

does it mention you in every possible way?

do let me know if it doesn't

because just like these sunsets,

I don't want to miss out anything from/with you

and even if I did, in a way I'll be happy

knowing we are infront of the same sunset

in different corners of the world

to witness the same sunset

where do we go now? by gracie abrams

let me know if we made it

that I can still hold your hand

that we can still dance on our favourite songs

because if we didn't make it out

that'll be a brutal way to die

knowing you were never beside me

that we missed all the sunsets

realising that I lost you

but I'll be happy, knowing that

every poem I wrote mentioned you

in every possible way

A City Away

a city away

meet me with van gogh

I hoped for such beginning

here's to love for believing

I, beside you

around the sadness to feel happy

a hand to hold, a kiss to remember

lying on the floor

while a world around becomes prettier

a day out in the city

a cup of coffee, a cup of tea

a view at night to see

early morning a train to catch

sleep on the floor by lumineers

let's leave this town so we can make it out

a city away

meet me with van gogh

a city that lives far away from us

but a place we have visited once

Yet it doesn't matter in love

as long as I have you beside me

around the sadness to feel pretty

a photo together, a hug to last long

a night out in the city

milkshakes and cupcakes

and a hint of stargazing

while you count the stars

and I, look at you while you do

a city away

meet me with van gogh

so I can meet you, my love

under the starry night

to experience what I always hoped for

for such beginning

here's to love for believing

Love Disfigured Me

Love disfigured me

But I saw it blooming with me

Love smiled at me from distance

In hope of something I'm yet to understand

It carried its own baggage of emotions

but made sure it took care of mines too

I saw love change into a fairytale

A tale that the love never believed in

And now lives it as its the only way to be alive

I saw love singing a change of heart by the 1975

and now it barely listens to it

Or maybe still does but secretly

I saw love broke my heart

but it had the right to else why would you call it love?

Love disfigured me

so I can try again to figure it out

love killed me

so I can be born again with same memories

love saw the most hardest way to be in love

as it never gave time to learn the easiest way

Love read books

and now barely gets time to read one

a thought at back of the mind

to go through with what is left to do

Love complains about less time

but lies around under a warm sheet

love visits my house in a day full of rain

but with only one umbrella to make it more romantic

crazy selfies, unexpected kisses and tight hugs

catches a cold, becomes dramatic

laughs it out, says it sucks

Love disfigured me

a room full of people but it only looked at me

a smile to go and mouths 'I love you"

If it wasn't for love, I wouldn't have a clue

a book full of handwritten poems

and a little drawings of favourite things

a sufjan stevens song to dance on

a coldplay song to sing

Love saw it can disfigured me

and yet can bloom

it held my hand, helped me to breathe

and gave my heart time to figure

with all the possibilities it can give

august

august began with rain

a poem on the horizon

one of the ways to go through the pain

august is here without you

like july said goodbye without you

a conversation of songs

and love, that's enough for the heart

I live in the hope of it all

as i didn't need anything more

like TS said "for me it was enough"

but to see you smile

to hold your hands

to take the candid pictures of you

to write a poem on your name

heart tries to live in the hope of it all

but it knows

august will slip away in the moment

like how homelands are taken away

a homeland that belongs to everyone else except me

cause you were never mine

October // 1

october misses you

the piano notes too

the photos on the wall,

the garden in your home

misses you like october does

words fell apart yet

you shared so much

come home now,

so I can tell you now

where I was?

but why did you ask

I'll never know now

Shiuli, I see you

blooming but for a short span

a span that felt like an infinity

meant to fall, like shiuli

Amma never forgets to say

take care of her,

take care of my shiuli

let her bloom so big

let her touch the sky

I see you shiuli,

I see you in my dreams

a place where we always meet

where I give you the flower

you always cherished

the flower that I cherished

so I'll meet you in our dreamland

where I will tell you where I was

while we wait for october to arrive

as it misses you too

just like how the piano notes too

as how I do, as how Amma do

so shiuli come home now

come home now as the

Mountain of flowers

awaits for you

october // 2

october arrives with your memories

a shiuli to be held in hands

a fragrance to never forget

but I've rarely met you this time around

a mind that is struggling to be calm and sound

october arrived but I'm yet to meet you

I'm forgetting your essence as the day passes by

I'm scared, shiuli

what if i lose october too?

what if i never get the chance to hold you?

a mountain of flowers, that's the dream, right?

what if i never make it?

a garden full of you, what if i never experience it?

But shiuli, you always gave me hope

a mountain of flowers, waiting for me

octobers to live, in your memory

so what if I don't get to see you,

a garden full of shiuli, that's what I'll have

a world with octobers will be a world with love

a thirty one days of unrequited hope and love

many of them to live, i have to make it

but whenever I'll meet you

meet me in a garden full of shiuli

on the first day of october

but till then, here's to your fragrance

that'll keep me alive

november

1st of november

october went with a smile

an october like that

I hardly remember

but now all I have is november

sweet, sweet november

it feels like home

and yet I feel far away from it

a feeling that I cannot express

that's what november is for me

so I'm curious, will I find out?

what november actually feels like

what my heart needs to feel like

for starters, why november feels like green

why do I feel like

it belongs to that colour out of all

but I know what I need from november

kindness, that's all

kindness to my heart

so I can figure out

what november actually feels like

as even if I'm fantasy parade

november comes closer to reality

a reality that I, out of all the seasons

belonged to november

in a frozen, cold time

where winter might come early

so I'm curious to find out

time is dancing by ben howard

and I'll make sure I'll have a laugh

before november,

opens the door for december

till then, lets go dancing

as we know we're only passing through

December

december arrived

with a baggage of emotions

carried upon his shoulders

and as december knows the most

whatever the heart went through

whatever the mind went through

It knows the most

now with only december to go

hope it feels kindness and love

because as the nights become cold and lonely

it'll need warm hug to live it through

you're on your own, kid by taylor swift

hold your hand, help yourself to breathe

I'm one step closer of surviving

the endless unknowing story

and I need/want to be here

to tell the tale

because i got not reason to be afraid

even if i'm on my own here

I'll hold it in, oh let's go dancing

as I do believe we're only passing through

in love again, now look who's laughing again

me again

back at you

hey love, can I hold your hand?

for a while?

as I missed the soft touch of your skin

If I could I will add the word forever

after the first line

But it's still a question that needs to be answered

So can I hold your hand?

But hey love, tell me this

how do you do it?

I wonder around the world

but find my home with you

I lose myself within thousands of words

but your name puts me back in the world

it all comes down to you

I come back at you

Sufjan steven wrote

Everything I feel returns to you somehow

and in the whole world

that's the only line I could understand

As it does returns me to you somehow

but this time

I'm only gonna let this be a wave of ocean

I'm glad that I didn't add the word forever

I'm way pass time where I ask, "is it too late"?

or maybe I'm wrong? As I am always

But this is known for forever now

As no matter what

my heart will feel love when it will see you

It will return to you somehow

forever

Even when my heart know it'll never deserve the love of yours

It'll return to you anyway

As for my heart,

holding your hand will be enough

So I come back to it

hey love, can I hold your hand?

just for a while?

tragedy

met you for first time at my house

and it never felt more safe than it ever did

songs in the background and a bowl of noodles

a hell lot of laughs and a whiteboard full of doodles

and yet it is a tragedy

only if i had the idea of where i could put all this love?

to let it drown or to let it be immortal?

to let your heart know or to write poems in your name?

either of them, it never made a difference

sleep on the floor by the lumineers

that could be the dream? right? my love?

all i ever did is, called you my love

but in person, the brain took over the emotions

and all the murmurations of words go silent in whisper

that if we can leave this town, we might make it out alive

a car, a bunch of clothes and you

that should be the dream, my love

and yet it is a tragedy

this life, it feels like its almost over

that I'm stuck in the same town

that'll never make it out alive

but you my love, you always meant to

so maybe in another life? next, probably?

how about next time, i meet you first at your house

and one day, I'll be waiting outside your house

a car, a bunch of clothes and you

and that would be the dream, my love

it won't be a tragedy then

I won't be fantasy parade then

I'll be be yours and you'll be mine

in next life, the murmurations of words

you'll hear them, loud and clear

your heart will know what i feel

It won't be just poems where i mention your name

and we will leave this town and we'll make it out alive

far away, where tragedy won't hit us

where we will grow old together

in a city where we will catch the subway together

where we will have a house of our own

a house where, a shelf full of unread books

old vcr and video tapes

where, songs will play in the background

a bowl of noodles,

and a whiteboard full of doodles

and you

In the next life, right my love?

answered and agreed

Am I Relapsing in your love?

"don't open that door now

You've come so far now"

Heart answered, mind agreed

Radio started playing ophelia

Mind uttered,"what do you want"?

But hey my rosemary,

Stay in my life that's all I want

I answered, heart agreed

Let me know how your heart feels

as I try to write this poem

"oh to be with you

oh how wonderful It will feel,

I'll meet you on 4th of July,

be mine in this wasteland

before either of us die"

So say what you feel

as I'll remember you always

Mind answered, I agreed

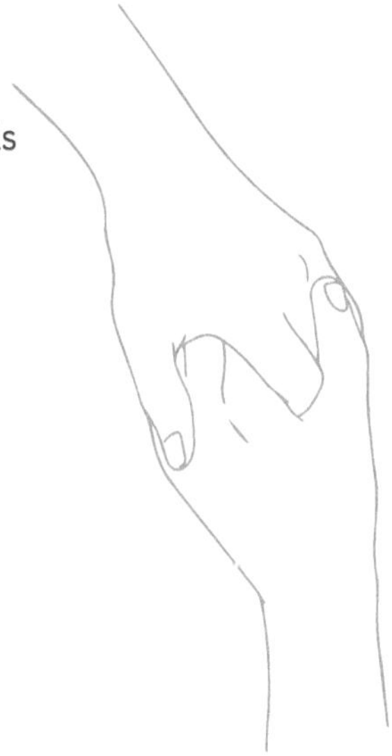

Vienna waits for you, my love

Vienna waits for you, my love

It awaits to hold you in her arms

"Oh she's so lucky"

While I'm stuck in

a loop of losing you

Vienna waits for you, my love

but she's asleep now in love

So the streets shared silence

but still whispered to adore you

So they can still remember you

Vienna waits for you, my love

As I'm stuck in a loop

I hope you meet at a sunrise

where the loop begins everytime

My love, Vienna waits for you

So I'll see you there

In her arms

the eyes have spoken

and haven't spoken a lot

the intensity grabs my attention

maybe it values more than love

your eyes have spoken

and haven't spoken a lot

as they show intensity

more than love

the endless conversations

and a sudden silence

somehow keeps the love

alive and yet your eyes

have spoken and

haven't spoken a lot

For me, they are the

pure definition

for my disfigured love

Is it the intensity again?

No dear, it's the love again

that keeps the intensity alive

as it all about your eyes and

how they have spoken and

haven't spoken a lot

Empty

1995, I first saw you
boarding the same train
(something I haven't told you yet)
I saw a glimpse of you
Felt I should talk to you
But I didn't, not yet
Now you know the
rest of the story
a day and night
dedicated by vienna
to out glory
I know we said
No calls, no letters
(It's depressing)
But I'm time traveling
just in case what if you wanted
a letter from me and I had none
Maybe we're supposed to
belong to each other
for a otherworldly night
in a unknown land
I'll hold you hand
but as vienna waits for us
as our own love stays
a mystery to us
but in a midst of
all of this as rumi said,
"somewhere beyond
right and wrong
there is a empty field
I'll meet you there, I'll meet you there

the light we lost

I'm a fantasy parade,

reality hits me differently

oh to be with you for a moment

fantasy becomes reality

Will I see you again?

you said no, sarcastically

A morning with breeze of rain

a small note for you,

"let's meet at our place"

as I cannot let this go in vain

July by far capsin

In a month of May

I asked you to hold a book

the light we lost by jill santopolo

hold it forever now, will you?

as the title goes,

you were my light and

I knew I have lost you

but hold on to it okay?

will you?

No,

she said,

sarcastically

pretty faces

the light we lost

came back to haunt us

scorched our hearts

in the dying wasteland

but the streams of rivers

knew our pretty faces

the face I have always

longed for to see smiling

back at me in love

and that's when I realized

the light I lost

never belonged to me

but today by far caspian

I wished to be

under the light

again and again

you're my

you're a shot of espresso
bathe in sunlight
but you've always been so much
for this heart of mine
a song that gets me through the day
you're the moonlight I reached for
but missed by infinity
you're the peace I always felt
my sadness that helped me
to love you even more
my reality that I always
saw slipping away
you're my poems that i cannot
explain to anyone else
you're my Martha that
I will always lose
you're my home that
I never return to but
will always longed for
you're my everything and nothing
and yet whenever i see you
all I could feel is how lucky
I've been to live this moment
with you, to exist with you,
all at the same time
and whenever I long for you,
all I see the sky hoping,
you're doing same
for us being under
the same sky

blue

I said, under the sky

meet me near the lake

you asked, where?

as the sky is limitless

and the lakes are dying

turning into a wasteland

so meet me nowhere

a place undying

made for me, made for you

that color us blue

where I'm a poet

and you're my words

reading out loud to you

but I'm a fantasy parade

trying to live out in a reality

that always disfigured me

but if I ever try to reach out

hold my hand, help to me breathe

as I'm tired of this endless loop

where I'm bound to lose you

so meet me near the lake

a nowhere to our love

that I pray for to be true

whisper of heart

the poet in me

never would've been borned

if it wasn't for you

lost in a wasteland where

my heart never would've found you

the whisper of heart

I guess they reached out to you

now my poems whisper your name

in hope that you heard them

and even if you haven't, try to,

as I will never stop writing them

ohh to write a poem beside you

the loud laughs and the shared silence

the being lost in your phone

and the sudden presence

the kind eyes and the soft hands

the unexpected smile

and the hug that is unplanned

what meaning my poems will have?

If it wasn't for you

So if you will, hold on to the

whispers of my heart

as they will always be

meant for you

I see you

under the kitchen lights

I saw you looking at me

and I wondered did you

caught me looking at you too?

the eyes tried to mention something

In hope of if you ever looked at me again

I'll tell you to not to look away

in the comfy silence, the chaotic sounds

It was 6.45 pm when you sat beside me

pulled out the book

which was meant to be yours

would you hold on to this?

well hold it forever, it is yours

the part where I say

this to you didn't happen

but the part where you get it did happen

and that's all I hoped for

where the moment became one for my poems to mention

Astoria by far caspian

You got yourself a milkshake to drink

which gave me some time to think

I'll write one for today

and one for another time

where we may meet

on the same street

but till then, read the book if you can

let me know if you can

as a bookstore is waiting for us

to be under its lights

in hope of I'll see you while you

looking at me

love is like a-

love is like a letter in bottle

thrown in a ocean in hope

to be found by the one you love

and we wait until it does

until we submerge into the water

rather than drowning we learn to swim

till it reaches its given path

love is like a dreamland

a place that makes your reality true

the reality where your love won

where it never disfigured you

where your only struggle

was to keep it alive

love is like a compartment

filled with each and every

emotions you go through

some stay, some stay under

the dust for being unnoticed

love is like a loop

keeps moving forward

yet stuck at one place

keeps coming back to us

love is like a sunday

that we wish to come early

and to wish it never meet the end

love is like sufjan stevens

that somehow makes everything

you feel return to the one you love

as the only thing that matters in the end

Is how your love stays alive

conversations

3 am, I passed by your home

wondered if you're still here

but how could you as the

world belonged to you

but as it was 3am

I remembered this time,

it belonged to us

middle of the night

through songs and texts

our conversations bloomed

the safest place on earth

that small or big texts

my words felt safe through them

a world that only belonged to us

a place that always remained us

conversations by far caspian

the topic for my another poem

and yet again, it all returned back to you

In hope of we never lose

this time, these conversations

and as I passed by your home

I received a text from you

And it's been months

since I received one

And I feared, if anything has changed

but apart from the distance

You and I, we were the same

got lost again in the convos

that made no sense,

you shared new songs you found

So I did the same

and I realised, no matter

what the distance is

You're one text away

even if you're away

we are still under the

same sky,

always

laundry and taxes

a poem in every universe

and thats all I could give

a hug that lasted longer

the holding of hands

and few words

thats all I could give

while you on the other side

introduced me to such love

I never thought I was capable of

a poem in every universe

for you where I wrote down

about the love i got from you

I'll lose you, one day, I know

and with everyday, losing you

comes closer to me but

it also brings this unexplainable

love that only a poem can take

the weight of and as I write it down

I realise, thats all I could give
a poem in every universe
where you're my martha
that I'm bound to lose
but i would've liked to
to just doing laundry and taxes
with you as everyday
I would've saw you
and I hope, a universe out there
exists in a space of reality
where I'm more than just words
where I'm yours and you're mine
and poetry lasts only for the sake of it
as if, you were mine and i was yours
I would've had more than words to give
and with the weight of love
where I get to realise
you're mine would've been the meaning I exists for
So I wouldn't mind if there's a
universe where we only do
laundry and taxes
as it would've been more than just
a poem in every universe
and I would've had you
to give you the absolute
all I could

composed

composed at heart
scorched at my feelings
I lost the freedom of who I was
Kept you close, kept you at heart
And yet I lost you
you're the heart
But so foolish of me
I thought it'll only belong to me
little freak by harry styles
A dying cry, a silent scream
I'll see you in my dream
but in reality, all alone,
and composed at heart
and I see you in love
In such a love I never expected
struggling to keep it alive
to keep it forever because
you're the heart
but will you see me, once?
let my head rest
on your shoulder, once?
hold my hand, once?
because you're the heart
and mine is getting composed
and it'll lose you for forever
If i lost myself too, for forever
so just you know
if you ever decide too,
I'll be waiting, for forever

me and new york // 1

look out the window

It's you and new york, now

how do you feel? I asked myself

how do I feel? I asked myself

I feel like I'm home

A home I never been to

A home I longed for

me and new york

perfect combination

breeze of the first rain

smell of the first coffee

first sunsrise at empire state

first sunset at brooklyn bridge

but why do I feel incomplete?

me and new york,

wasn't that the dream?

so why it feels like

as in a poem has been ended

abruptly In the middle of it

me and new york // 2

christmas came early

a rooftop full of snow

and i saw a couple dancing

through my opened window

a view I witness rarely

a view prettier than art of van gogh

carrie and lowell by sufjan stevens

played while the couple danced

and new york felt like home again

where my heart ached

for the touch of her fingers

which I used to hold as we danced

but now those are the faded stories

that I wake up from, dreaming

in hope for them to be reality again

but now its just me and new york

smiling at each other

while new york snows for me

I write my stories for her

"24 july, new york 2028

christmas came early

a rooftop full of snow

and I saw a couple dancing

through my opened window"

and as the story goes by

new york changes seasons for me

and now I'm already waiting for

autumn to show up, in a hope for

this time I'll be one dancing

in someone else's story

"do I have to lose you too?"

love. How did i know it existed?

How did I know it existed for me?

I knew it existed the second I saw you

Before you I always wondered

with you, I always experienced it

your arms in my arms

those surprising forehead kisses

that late night poems that you sent

that I always saw in the morning

making my day

the tight hugs

the catching of eyes

from the long distance

your "I'm always here"

while you holded my hand

To my "hold my hand, help me to breathe"

you always kept me safe with your love

That's how I knew. Love, It existed

it existed for me, by you, from you.

Now that you've gone,

to the stars where you belong

I never saw the andromeda so happy

but leaving me unanswered to my

hold my hand, help me to breathe

Now all I have is pictures of yours

where I see you smiling back at me

the day I lost you, I asked myself

"do I have to lose you too?"

the one last kiss that could've lasted longer

the things that I would've done differently

And you would've been right beside me

so I ask myself now

who would hold my hand? who would help me to breathe?

and I remembered the song you shared

gone, gone, gone by phillip phillips

that gave my heart a relief

that even thou, I lost you

you will always be mine to love

and that, I'm never gonna lose

home // 1

came home and

I realised I was alone

Called out your name

"Gwen?" And the silence haunted me

but I call out your name In hope

that maybe one day

you'll say my name again

"I'm here pete"

I came home and I saw picture

of us lying on the floor

"all the things I could've done differently"

I said to myself

all the things I could've done differently

and you would've been beside me

but home, that was never a place

it's you gwen, my home, where I rested

where I knew my heart is safe, I am safe

Lately III by coin

and you were all I needed

now the home is too quiet

It misses your smile

the kisses on forehead

the wall in my bedroom

misses all the candid photos

we never got the chance to take

why did I have to lose you too?

for the promise I made but couldn't keep

you were all I needed, for a second

only to lose you forever in time

now I have a place to sleep

but not a home to rest

as all I ever needed you

for second, as a home

you were all I needed

home // 2

among a lot

we mattered for few

a place turned into home

wait, no no

people who became home

in a short period of time

lived few moments

that felt like an infinity

a glass of beer or

a cup of coffee

just tell us when and where

and We'll be there

Isn't this like a

movie you loved

but it ended before

you could know

but Isn't time a bitch?

the unpredictable magic ever

you could see it passing

but could never know how

or maybe we were busy enough

making the most of it unknowingly

and now the time we lived on

the time we dreamt of are

two different things

where in the first

we felt happy

and in the second one

we want to be

home // 3

i miss home

season of rain

a terrace full of flowers

where waking up early felt like living

a terrace full of memories

time is dancing playing in the background

manifestations of dreams

a place to scream

i miss home

a room full of people

people i love the most

noodles and wine

night full of dance

a photoshoot to be held

I almost forgot how all of it felt

I miss home

Especially myself

the kid who had no fear

who never felt lost in the world

who knew what his heart wanted to say

but now, daydream delusional

a fantasy parade

finding it hard to trust

a price the heart had to pay

a heart that doesn't know anymore what to say

overwhelmed by life

I guess that's how adult life feels like

anxiety attacking, mind crumbling and a long sigh

but if I've been lost and found myself before

Is it for poems to recite, stories to write and so much more

i do miss home

a terrace full of people

people i love the most

laughs and sound in every corner

fights and sad faces too

plate full of noodles

a whiteboard and doodles

maybe i can't go back to live it again

but i can so relive it again

I miss home

dances and glances

apart from home, meet up at new places

now it feels like miles away

a new home near by

again laughs, dances and cries

in hope of it comes back to me

that home comes back to me

because i miss it

home // 4

a cup of coffee on the table

and i saw the stain of a spilled coffee

reminds me of you everyday

No, i have not cleaned it

i am a fool in love, yes but not stupid

any part of you that i find

I'll keep it for as long as it could be there

reminds me the nights we spent

a kitchen full of love

a bowl of spaghetti, a glass full of chocolate milkshake

radio ga ga on the loop and you

made me fall in love again and again

oh love, i want to be in love again with you

to feel your fingers through my hair

an assurance to fall asleep on your lap

a way to show kindness through our doings

All of it, in our own world

where we made a home for ourselves

where our eyes will meet each other

where we'll dance on any song

a place where you promised me to grow old together

and here i am, alone in the kitchen full of love

a bowl of spaghetti, a glass of chocolate milkshake

radio ga ga, all of it, is here but not you

now i miss the kindness in a world full of cruelty

now i miss the assurance in a world full of anxious

i was and will always be a fool in love

but was i stupid too? To believe in the promise?

now, who will prove me wrong?

for which i seek you and the world has lost you

so where can i go anyway?

a friend asked me to go back home

now how do i tell him? its just walls and empty spaces

an empty bowl, an empty glass

a music player turned into junk

and an empty cup on the table

homeland // 1

one more poem on calling you my homeland

a place where i found solace

i am too late to love you now

yet a solace exists in the love i have

but i am too late to be in love with you now

only if i was not late

you, me and new york would've been the dream

it still is, but new york without you

it'll call out your name, it will scream

only if i was not late

I would've made it out alive from this town

a car, bunch of bags, deposited money and you

ben howard on the loop

lumineers sneaking in between

tell me, is this what a homeland means?

a person but home

but if you reach late to your home

the fear of it being taken away exists

and you're my homeland

that's where i lost you

that's where i made myself late

a destiny where I'm destined to lose you

because i remember what darwish said

homelands are taken away

so what if i was never late?

would you still be here?

for the dream? you, me and new york

for the road trip? don't forget your spectacles

would all this be possible?

only if i was not late

but i promise, I'll be there at the other side of the road

in next life, you'll be my homeland again

a house of our own

garden in the backyard

plums and strawberries

bicycles with a basket

bookshelves and vinyl player

a homeland I'll be destined to keep to myself

a person I'll never lose

a place I'll never be late too

homeland // 2

my heart reached out to you

whenever it mentioned your name

a song to share every day

and I'm making sure

I never runout from those

but to be honest, for this moment

I had no poem in mind

but mahmoud darwish had different plans

as he said he called his love

homeland out of ignorance

not realizing they are taken away

and here I am, too, calling you my homeland

a place where I feel safe and sound

where my words can live in silence,

and still have a meaning

a place where I might be at rare times

to feel your presence, your hugs

the touch of your hands and your smiles

So I guess that's how a homeland feels like

where I do get to see you,

but with a price that I have to pay

so it doesn't matter now what I say

you're destined to be my homeland

a part of me that my heart will cherish

but will never get to live with it

so for now, I hope,

you'll never be anyone's homeland

but rather a place they can return to

where you will be witnessed

with your flaws and love

as the only flaw of yours anyone can experience

is your absence in their lives

so never be anyone's homeland

but a place where they can return

because when they do,

they return to you

hold my hand, help me to breathe

let me ease with my own words

falling apart again as the mind struggles

I woke up tired

as the eyes see a faded picture

It'll be alright I told myself

as it fumbles more

hold my hand, help me to breathe

held my own hand and helped myself to breathe

a poem, a story, heart got the words to write

But my mind asks me, is it right?

a lack of vacancy I sensed

worried, that's how I felt

woke up everyday in the same sense

but wrote it down today

as it made more sense

But i guess, It's just a matter of time

a time passes by and a time comes by

I'll still be here, as life unfolds more

and I'll make sure,

that the heart rests,

and the mind got vacancy

for the thoughts that can be turned into stories

as when I'll be gone,

that's all I will leave behind

stories

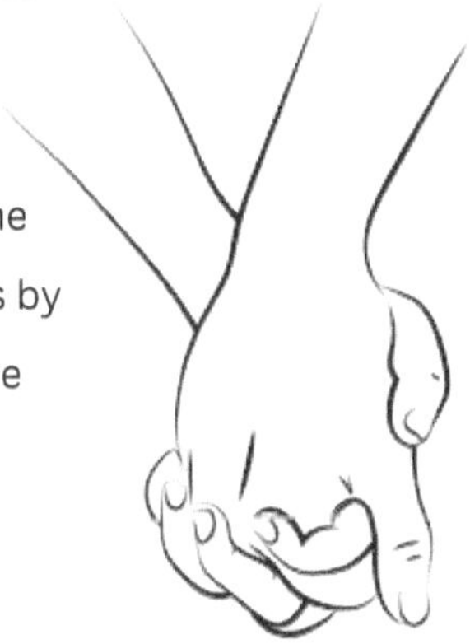

young love

I looked out the window

In hope of seeing you

and there were you

already looking at the window

hoping I'll be looking at you too

our eyes have met beyond times now

they know what we feel

you texted me as you got in the car

"cheese cake and milkshake in the fridge"

And I texted back

"the one you bake? and the one you made?"

you smiled at me and drove away

you turned on the radio

and it played flowers in your hair by the lumineers

you told me immediately as you reached home

as it was their concert where we first met

on cleopatra, our eyes met

while ophelia came along

our voices synced together

"heaven help a fool who falls in love"

and to the sleep on the floor

we made sure we made out of the town

and as you reached your bed to rest

I wonder, now whats next?

a young love of us

far away from each other

a subway to catch

or a drive to go on

a shy kiss

a long hug

And before we meet each other again

I'll make sure I'll be at the window

to see you already looking at me

Mountain fairy

a mountain full of dreams

also lives near by them

drives at midnights

a escape from reality

unconditional at its best

and I hope to meet her, under the purple skies she loves

a cup of tea, a bowl full of maggi

taylor swift and one direction in the background

where we do the thing that introduced us

stargazing in his memory

creating constellations as we see one by one

Time is dancing by ben howard

to realise we're just travellers

passing through from this life

wired to each other by so many things

to laugh it out on some of them

so a poem on you as you deserve more

as moonlight reaches the surface of earth

I'm happy it reaches even more closer

that from around the world

I got be a part of your world

where stars rests easy in open

where they shine the most

and I happen to believe

you could be one of the reason

why they do what they do

mentioning you

It's been some time since I wrote a poem,

I wonder what kept me away from writing one,

you? No, I don't think so

Because I'm being away from you longer than a poem i haven't written

busy I'll say, but my heart won't agree

as it still thinks about you

about how it fell out of love for you

I wondered, was that even possible?

a heart that mentioned you whenever possible

now as fade, as it gets, heart mentions you less

and now, for this time, my heart does not feel like a mess

yess, it finds hard to love

but it is love

I'll need time, it'll need time

to mention someone under a pink sky

where I'll hold hands and wouldn't feel shy

but like I said, it'll need time, I will need time

and for now, heart smiles with no pain

it helps to keep my mind sane

sun room by far caspian

a poem after a while

wrote with a smile

hoping I wouldn't be away from you for a long time

but mentioning you always, I don't need that time

and I know, it's unpredictable and unknown to me

so if I mention you less, my heart might lose the habit

habit of yours

where sufjan steven's songs are just songs

and everything I feel, does not come back to you

because when it does,

all it feels a void, with no end, all alone

which starts to make me feel, all alone

so if I mention you less, I might lose the habit

and that void will become brighter

where I'm not alone

so hoping, love finds me to the other side of it

as i know, it disfigures me,

only to figure me out

so tell me what is it?

a crowded room

and my eyes met your eyes

making me realise

why I've been born in this universe

so my heart can know how to love

and to know how love feels like

A summer morning

a cup of coffee

and dancing with you in the kitchen

to whatever song radio plays

A passionate kiss

after we watch a romantic movie

or it can be a book

what counts is the taste of your lips

plums and strawberries

A road trip out to the country

around the mountains

where the sun shines for us

and stargazing as we lay down

under the stars for constellations to count

A love where I can rest easy

crumbling thoughts won't hurt

where eyes speak kindly,

assuring the safety of heart

so maybe that's why

In a crowded room

my eyes met your eyes

making me realise

why I've been born in this universe

to love you so my heart can stay kind

so it can rest easy under your love

but tell me if it's real or

am I going to wake up?

because I'd rather not

not in a time where I'm not yours

and your love is not my home

to rest easy

so tell me what is it?

love,

I'll like to die by your bare hands
oh what are you waiting for?
a kiss on the forehead
and I'm straight to hell
hell because I lost your love in this life
a life where I found love
that felt like a blessing
like the first smell of rain
like when ben howard sings
a love where I knew I was at peace
sweet kiss on the lips to save the day
a love where you were my prayer that i wished to be true
a love where new york felt like a home
as I rested myself in your arms
a home within a home
a love I have lost but strong enough
that it makes me believe
I'll find you again, in another life
with hope of you being my prayer again
and I wishing it to be true again
but for this life, as I saw love disfigured me
I saw you in love,
that made me believe in a motion that is unconditional
that i don't need to have a place in your heart to love you
I, having a place in my heart for you is and will always be enough
and as long as I'm here, breathing,
my heart will value that place
it'd value you for what you are
and that, is
love

grow old

will I grow old?
I don't wanna know
a heart that has been already sold
who does it belong to?
I think you know
but will I grow old without you?
it scares me to even imagine
but here as a young one
I already know the answer
we'll won't be a part of our lives
so many summers will pass away
a few songs to make us remember
you won't be mine, and I'll still be yours
two corners of the world,
far away from each other
and you won't be mine, but I'll still be yours
my silence will grow faster than me
words will go blank, and all will remain
staring into each other's eyes
but I'm glad even with the silence
there will be no lies
between us
we'll meet surely at parties
two corners of the same place
a room full of crowd
I'm hoping now that our eyes will meet
a smile will exist into that one moment
and I'll start walking towards you

but I know I'm growing old without you
so a few glasses of wine to empty
as we talk life till the silence hits again
and I see you drifting away
like a summer pass away
a universe so cruel
for introducing me to such love
such love that I'm destined to let it go
such love where I'm supposed to grow old
in a place where i won't make you smile
or hear you laugh
or see you dance
and everything a love holds in its meaning
but i guess that's my part of love that won't experience you
but love will experience you
it will see you do all of it
It will see you grow old with it
and while it does,
I'll be at the other side of the world
hoping to grow old
so i can see you for one last time
in/with love
so I hope, i do grow old

end of the affair

summer passed away
and I miss how love feels like
I'm sure I'll come back to it
the soon I see you
but I can say I know how it sounds like
Ben howard on shuffle
it's new to me, this feeling
a motion of it exists because of you
but I'm missing out on you
so his voice got me covered
but with every new song
the feeling for love changes
the melodies and his words
creates a world for me
where I experience your love
but as soon as I hear end of the affair
"Now I watch her
running around in love again"
these words help me to live the reality
a reality where I do miss you
where I miss asking you all my silly little things
but now,
My words are fumbling
as they try to speak to you
Slowing me down to the point
where I got nothing to say
where it seems like it's the

end of the affair by ben howard

but I guess it's okay

because these lines by him

"Now I watch her

running around in love again"

makes me the most happiest too

As knowing you being in love

makes you happy too

so hold on to it as long as you can

figure it out, as love figures you out too

and lastly, love,

as the sun will shine will tomorrow

start your day with ben howard

hoping it'll make the rest better

as we might never know how much time

we got for ourselves

so before it passes away

listen to love

As for me, it could be the only way

to reach your heart

where if not me, my love will atleast rest,

knowing it does have a place with you

in your heart

moonraker

a poem comes to my mind
as I Listen to moonraker by ben howard
love, you do make things easy
ask me if you're ever in doubt
poems on your name
and my hearts sings out the words in ease
while I stay in love and kind
and I know you wouldn't mind,
would you?
for me to write poems in your name
because then I'm immortal in a way
well at least my love will be
through the words i sing along
and i ask you, to join me along
would you?
for me to write poems in your name
as you sit beside me with those kind eyes
and making everything look so easy
so a poem for now and a poem for then
you and I, wish we could go through together
as you and I, are both moonrakers
so Let's dance to it
and my heart knows, you'll make it
would you?
a poem comes to my mind
for me to write on your name
as this one just like many others
waiting to be written
on your name

verb

so many sayings left unsaid

a lot of musings, so many characters

to read out loud and to experience

but now a void remains here

for you to be a traveler

around the andromeda

while the surface misses your touch

but you're in a place that understands you

what more could anyone ask for?

to be understood, that is all we seek

Vincent by don mclean

but I could have told you, verb

"This world was never meant for one

as beautiful as you"

and now you're the starry night

Undying, on every part of this world

a art that will remain in poems and stories

so verb, make the moon your home

as you always wished to be

meanwhile, down here,

the hearts around the world who love you

will cherish you and your art

until the end of time

troubled

Troubled to the core

I don't see an easy way out of here

and as the night goes on

I find solace in my own thoughts

a poem to be written, for me?

hold my hand, help me to breathe

anxiety lives on throughout the day

peace breathes in a lonely night

This seems to be a sad poem, isn't it?

but it's a mixed emotion of both

happy and sad

now how is that possible?

That's what I have to figure out

time is dancing by ben howard

To believe we're only passing through

I'll laugh as the day and night go on

anxious

away from the chaos

I'll run away in a heart beat

but my legs are anxious enough to lose

mind tries to forget it

heart creates a mountain of unsaid words

where am I going wrong?

some days are under the stars

and some are the suicide letter of van gogh

ben howard's words keeps me alive

a possibility of a dream I see

days of new york in love

so even with the anxious legs

I will have to run away , and no, not from myself

but to find myself, and in that moment

as a rainy day appears

these anxious legs will dance

mind will try to make a memory of it

and heart will create a mountain for it

turning the chaos into a starry night

where the letter will cease to exist

ben's words will still be here

and the dreams will be reality

days in new york with love

i wish you were here

mountain fairy

roaming bird

sunsets and drizzles

i wish you were here

skies would've been different

i wish you were here

rainbows to witness

ben howard and you

a cup of tea and you

a cafe to go to

musings and letters to write

an escape that'll feel right

under the moonlight

stars, moon and you

runaway, come home

but you're my mountain fairy

sunsets and rainbows

drizzles and grey clouds

how could it can be left behind?
an escape that'll feel right
a place that will feel right
london with love
new york for love
a home in between
a garden full of sunflowers
peaches and strawberries
a home with safe and sound
rooms full of posters and collectibles
hall full of no fear of coming late

It's okay, I'll wait

but to make sure, you stay mountain fairy

a view from the window

a ride to the nearest hill

bicycles to run

I know you wouldn't mind

in a weather full of wind

weathering with you

as I'll only ever need you more than any blue sky

and if you ask, why?

start from the beginning

you're my mountain fairy

sunsets and drizzles to witness

while i witness you

in hope of it all

where i know love won't disfigure me

where i know my gwen will be here

no fear of losing

knowingly, unknowningly

so if you ask, why?

start from the beginning

read the poem out loud

while i end it with saying

my mountain fairy

i wish you were here

i wish you were here

I'll ask her everyday - how?

a waterfall of kindness

I'll ask her everyday - how?

her heart breathes love like it beats to live

tell me what you are?

a waterfall of kindness?

a restaurant of manifestations?

Then yess i know that!

but tell me more?

they say you haven't lived enough

Ask me and I'll let them know

the basket full of memories you carry

oh to be a witness for all of them

I'll let them know you're a storyteller

a memory told by you

a moment to live with you

but tell me more?

an old soul

by mind, by heart

a mind of so many worlds

lived, unlived

a heart of so many words- said, unsaid

an honest conscience

I'll ask her everyday - how?

but what i do know?

busy hands, subtle hands

clumsy around, always around

an unexpected laugh, a known laugh

faithful by heart

a heart that misses home
a heart that belongs to mountains
an admiration to aspire
an inspiration to admire
a care to take, a care to show
I'll ask her everyday - how?
because i do want to know more
with everyday passing by
as how season change
While all you do is sit beside her
in silence and in sound
at sunset, at dawn
In a night full of drizzle
let her know everyday
ask her everyday
how? how? how?
for a heart to be this kindful?
for a heart to be this liveful?
for a heart to be this loveful?
let her know, ask her
everyday

fall out of love

let me know

when can i fall out of love with you?

because my mind has no idea at this point

a memory i already made even before i could live it with grace

that's what my head is right now, a complete mess

a sufjan stevens song to rescue

and it misfired on my love

oh my love, to forget you completely

do i really have to love you completely?

why such a paradox to exist?

within days, i knew, for you i was a misfit

but a hopeless romantic heart had a different plan

so i wished, i'll make my heart cruel if i can

but a mention of your name

a poem on your name

listening to a song on your name

makes me do all the things i just mentioned

as in there is no tomorrow

but wait? there is no tomorrow isn't there?

a tomorrow without you is the same as

a world without ben howard

a world without tay's august

a garden where flowers never bloomed

a place where I'm doomed

so please do let me know,

when can i fall out love with you?

because if i don't, I'll have to love you more than I've known you

but i guess I'll do that anyways

a love for you forever

only to lose you amongst the world

a corner of the world for you

where I'll ask the rest of the world about you

and a corner of the world for me

where poems on your name will be written

to keep you closer with every poem

So let me know,

when can i fall out love with you?

will you?

my love, would this be hard to live?

neon lights, a motel to spend the night

a long way away from home

a black volvo, old cassettes & you

under the vast blue sky

still driving under a moonlight sky now

oh love, would this be hard to live?

my love, lets listen to the lumineers

lets get out of the town

so we can make it out

savings enough to build a home

a home, a dream and you

a home with a room for workspace

pages on the ground with your unfinished chapters

while i write poems on every situation

a story to tell, a story to live

oh love, would this be hard to live?

betterment in understanding

learning through the phases

for each other and by each other

when you're around, you're the one

my love, all mine, all mine

but when you're not around

It'd still be you, cause my love, all mine, all mine

while away, hand written letters to share

phone calls to hear each other's voices

oh love, would this be hard to live?

It'll be isn't it?

then i guess it's time to wake up

wake up from a dream that lasted a poem

a poem on your name that seeks you and only you

longs for a love you'll give because no other comes close

oh love, would this be hard to live?

wake me from bleachers

only if i could capture your heart

let me know if ever i did

because if i did, I'll hope it won't be a dream

but it is, isn't it?

a dream to be a reality

where you're mine and I'm all yours

where you do complete your story

and still keep writing poems on every situation

while we drive under a moonlight sky

away from home, away from everyone

my love, would this be hard to live?

while you remain beside me?

I don't think so it'll be

because if we do leave the town

we'll make it out

alive

my van gogh letter

you were my van gogh's letter

wait...

you are my van gogh's letter

but the one that made me live

to see you each day

and as seasons changed

spring, i fell in love

winter, still there

but now i see my way out

this is the part i hate the most

I'll remember you more than I've known you

that i see you everyday

but i could never be yours

that i found home in you

but i couldn't make a place there

it all sounds sad but trust me, my love, it doesn't

a heart knows how to love and it did exactly that

you are my van gogh's letter for a reason

and especially the one that made me live

so what if i lose you?

I was destined to

i made you my homeland

and homelands are meant to be taken away

seasons will change

summer will be without you

a sunny morning I'll be thinking about you

a poem on your name for forever

a poem where you will live till I'll live and beyond that

a hug to have, a kiss to be missed

a song that'll never be the same

but you'll be here as a home that i lost

and I'll be here, to grieve that loss

so do know it'll be me if you ever recieve a letter

unknowingly knowingly i hope you'll know

a nameless letter mentioning you

just like how van gogh mentioned sadness in his letters

just like that I'll mention you but in love

because you are my van gogh's letter

where you made my heart felt alive

more than it ever could,

in love

screams of rain

your name flashed on my phone's screen

like a thunderstorm among the clouds

I bet you heard them too?

screams of rain in love

will you dance with me in rain?

as that might keep us sane

half way in october

autumn stays in my heart

and whenever it rains

It reminds me of your soft heart

about you by the 1975

I miss your face as a memory

a memory that I'm trying to keep alive

until I see you

But now I'm worried

worried of missing you

more than loving you

and as the rain stops

and the sky becomes blue clear

I'll miss you even more

just like a perfect summer dream

but that is yet to come

As of now, the rains have conquered their place

and the screams of rain grow more louder

so until it slow downs

I'll write more poems in love

in hope of one day the rains will stop

And we will witness a blue sky

and the blue sky witnesses us

wasteland, baby

lying on my bed

while my heart listens to

wasteland, baby by hozier

my mind feels like

a empty box

a box full of vacancy

but I can assure it

won't look the same

when it comes to feel things

my mind is alone and yet

all these people live in it

my mind is like a

wasteland and hozier

explains it beautifully

it's 1.57 am as I write

down this line only to realise

it's 1.58 am as I keep

continue to write

am I fantasy parade?

or just a little sane one?

both ways, it helps me

to write, to love and to feel

it's 2.00 am now and

I got up from the bed

to look at the night sky

and it was clear and

I could see jupiter

looking back at me

and as the song played

"that's the wasteland, baby"

I am amazed at my existence

to be able to exist in this

wasteland where the only

scorched place is hearts

of poets who are awake

at 2.05 am, looking in hope

at the night sky that even

the scorched place will bloom again

flowers will grow, love will grow

and We'll back how we were before

as poets of worlds, to write poems

in love, for love and by love

fantasy parade

Baby I'm a fantasy parade

worlds collide in my heart

love feels lost within them

and yet the hand reaches out to you

And in the midst of this chaos

my heart got to know now

in a world full of emptiness

It'll feel whole again beside you

in a world full of crowd

It'll feel at home and safe beside you

Sweetcake and milkshakes

sunset, you and some coldplay

bicycle rides or maybe long walks

with few polaroids of candid moments

and a few long lasting talks

but baby I'm a fantasy parade

a hopeless romantic in love

existing for love, existing for you

to feel your hand on my head

as I rest it on your shoulder

while the skylight turns to moonlight

and we just lay in each other arms

now tell me is it too much?

and if it is, then tell me,

why love feels as such?

bathed in sunlight

a shot of espresso

the first smell of rain

maybe because I'm fantasy parade

but baby let me tell you

I am not a fantasy parade

I'm just a dreamer trying to

make this dream of mine

a reality that is nothing but

a fantasy written in books

and made in movies

and sang in songs

in the end, only to exist

as a reality among us

my poetry answers

my poetry answers to you

speaks to you in words

I never could speak of

It allows me to hide there

a place where I am yours

a place that felt like home

But if my poetry answers

Have you ever asked anything?

and the answer always

ripped one flower from my heart

when I was hoping for a garden to bloom

in a place I never belonged to

I realised my poetry was

answering in a wrong place too

But what about the garden now?

Can a new place for it grow?

august by taylor swift

but even now i'm trying to slip away

like august did as you were never mine

but as my poetry answers anyway

it never tried to understand

what the questions are

as it only hoped for

to be understood

so it'll bloom anyway,

let summer go,

and let autumn come

It'll still bloom,

as my poetry will always answer

under the stars

mountain of dreams
suffered at my feelings
all I had these silence screams
hold my hand, help me to breathe
heart ached, mind remained busy
poems and edits to cope
I'm tired to write one
I'm tired to make one
but it kept the mind busy
heart still ached
ached for stars,
remember our favourite batch?
the favourite five
a sight to feel
a time where I heal
but I'm a fantasy parade
how could I possibly heal?
If I never lived to live
in another life by son lux
where I wish my other one
lives in reality and the what ifs
are happening but not
shoved under the fear
where the screams are louder
and my feelings bloomed

and the mountains of dreams
do come closer each moment
and where I rest my eyes easy
under the stars knowing
they'll be here when I open them

run away with me, my dear

Sat next to you

whispered "run away with me"

"what?" you said

my heart ached and

the words remained silent

Nothing, I said

but run away with me

to the place you want to

a place that will love you too

from grocery buying to

finding new places to eat

the place will fall in

love with you too

sleep on the floor by lumineers

a garden in the backyard

a basket full of plums

breadsticks and wine

And a window view

where you can see

the sun shine

so will you run away with me, my dear

to the place you want

a place that you'll love too

cause if we never leave this town

we might never make it out

your name

to send out letters

without a address

I was suprised enough

that I even wrote them

But they did had a name

so I kept writing them

as saying your name out loud

while writing it became my

favourite thing about me

heyy with your name

A basket full of dreams

where I called out your name

a moment turned back in time

I saw you looking at me

an unambiguous love

in a dreamland where

you're mine and I am yours

but I hate waking up to reality

where the basket full of dreams

has no meaning and where

you're not mine to be called for

where your name is the

prayer i say in silence and

wish it to be true someday

but heyy with your name

till then, if we could,

if I could

call you by my name,

let me know

by calling me by your name

new york

Christmas night hangout
I was all by myself with you
I had a state of mind
woke up next morning
in your arms freezing with you
these times by far caspian
daydream delusions
tell me newyork
do you dreamt about me?
as i did and I loved how I lived it
a cold breeze of rain in the morning,
brooklyn calling me out in love,
to a disfigured love
it reminded me of her
a thought was shared with her
"you, me and new york"
a thought that became a dream
which ended with being a empty void
yet I had you, in sleepless nights

yet I had you, in sleepless nights
with writing poems without a rhyme
without her, alone with you
tell me it won't feel like a crime?
christmas night hangout
I was all by myself with you
I had a dream state of mind
woke up next morning
in a reality where you yet to
happen my reality
new york? wait for me okay?
okay

milkshakes // 1

daydream delusional

baby, I'm a fanstasy parade

In hope that

I'll read out my poems to you

that I wrote for you

but can I ever do that?

but hey, don't answer that

let it happen if it ever does

as whatever I do,

it always comes back to you

the only thing by sufjan stevens

and I wrote a poem named

Sweetcakes and Milkshakes

but I'll wait if that's I'm meant to do

a traveler, finding his path

but wait for me, if you're meant to do

both disguised in unshared love

but I'll meet you halfway

as giving up on you

means I'll lose myself

so hold on to me if you will

as I'm yet to read my poems to you

that I wrote for you

milkshakes // 2

daydream delusional

baby, I'm a fanstasy parade

between days by far caspian

sunset arrived late for us

I've came this far in love

but for your or my own sake?

sweet cakes and milkshakes

hold my hand, help me to breathe

an a angel that seemed sweet

I'm not lost anymore in you

but was never found by you

don't you want to know now?

where I belong now?

dancing by the window view

the songs I played, you knew a few

don't you know by now?

maybe that's how it could be now

so if you ever get lost

come find me

come find me

superbia at the night cafe

I say, a dying world, full of hate

while I'm here, holding a mic

with words full of love that

no one cares to understand

I say, a dying world, full of hate

"oh hello figured love, we haven't met"

I mean, how can anyone have met

a love that has been figured with no hate

I say, a dying world, full of hate

a Poet and a king

one assembled by thoughts,

one by soldiers,

yet share the same outcome

death.

I say, a dying world, full of hate

In a Night cafe, all alone, I bait

I won, the bait.

I say, a dying world, full of hate,

Meet me love, in the streets of Italy

but let me warn, a Poet with love is deadly

disfigured me now, don't surprise me

As I say, a dying world, full of hate,

I'll still cherished my disfigured love,

I bait

poetry, fiction and me // 2

3.33 am

dinner & diatribes on loop

and the mind is again

not vacant anymore

my thumbs start to write

but never get it right

my mind is a fantasy parade

a poem is waiting to be written

and it's not 3.33 am anymore

dinner & diatribes still on loop

"thats the kind of love, I've been dreaming of"

a dreamland in my mind was born

to touch the love I yet to see

in the reality of the worlds

but I woke up again,

in the middle of the night

started narrating all the poetry

I can think of in my mind

poetry, fiction and me

maybe that's all I need to survive

but as I realised, this poem

does not belong to fiction

but to the reality I am in

3.44 am now

still on the loop and I asked my self,

what kind of love do

you dream of anyway?

and all my heart did is,

it took her name

and here I am again,

going into the fiction

where my love stays alive

in hope for her and with

how the time passes by

and the very end comes near

the fear of me hoping for it forever

haunts me in every sense

It's 4.00 am and I didn't even realise

when my mind stopped focusing

on the song except the part

"thats the kind of love, I've been dreaming of"

Now, this, this may not be a poem

but more of words I wrote that

my mind had the sense of

and that's how I knew,

poetry, fiction and me

might not have to be

the case everytime

Oh, if you've read it till here

wait for few seconds

as the song will end

and I'll rest my eyes,

with the thought of

"thats the kind of love, I've been dreaming of"

This one is for the ones who have a keen eye for

details! If you've gone through all the poems -

almost every poem had a song mentioned in it!

So you may have reached the end of the book

but you can continue your fantasy parade with the

playlist created by every song within the poems!

Scan below to continue your journey!

Thanks to everyone who kept motivating me for this but a very, very special thanks to Mahesh Mali, who helped me throughout this whole thing. From advising on how to make my poems more better to adding illustrations in the book!

From one poet to another, thank you!

This book consists all the poems I've written so far (well not all of them). That's for another book i guess but with 2024, the journey for my next book starts!

9 798896 738657